SITELESS

SITELESS

1001 Building Forms

François Blanciak

The MIT Press
Cambridge, Massachusetts
London, England

This book was set in Helvetica Neue by the MIT Press and was printed and bound in the United States of America.

Library of Congress Cataloging-in-Publication Data

Blanciak, François.
Siteless : 1001 building forms / François Blanciak.
    p.   cm.
ISBN 978-0-262-02630-7 (pbk. : alk. paper)
1. Architecture—Composition, proportion etc.   2. Form (Aesthetics)   I. Title.
NA2760.B52   2008
721—dc22   2007015858

11

CONTENTS

ACKNOWLEDGMENTS

This book has been prepared in various countries: China, Denmark, the United States of America, and Japan, over the course of the last five years. Only in its final stage could I focus on this work full-time.

Hence, I have to first thank the Japanese government for subsidizing my first years in Tokyo as an independent researcher by providing me with a fellowship. It is surprising that one of the most unaffordable and supposedly chaotic cities in the world turned out to be the most stable environment for gathering and developing my ideas.

Debt is also owed to my former employers; Aaron Tan, Bjarke Ingels, Peter Eisenman, and Frank Gehry, for enabling me to develop my work on the side from different urban locations and diverse dogmatic approaches. Yet, in the serial, crafted, and *siteless* nature of this study, a greater deal of inspiration comes from the architects Iakov Chernikhov, John Hejduk, and Hermann Finsterlin.

A number of individuals have also either encouraged or questioned my work with sharp criticisms, and pushed me to enhance its quality. Among them (in no specific order): Ali Tabatabai, Napoleon Meraña, Yoram Lepair, Michael Sorkin, Aida Mirón, Masashi Nagamori, Leopoldo Sguera, Tom Russotti, Vytautas Baltus, Tynnon Chow, Amadou Tounkara, and Siri Johansen managed to formulate constructive comments. In addition, the insights of Michael Wert and André Moore Guimond have been helpful in the editing of my manuscript.

Finally, I must avow that the physical condition of Tokyo—a city that threatens to collapse at any time—is what forced me to publish this rather venturesome oeuvre without further delay.

F. B., Tokyo, January 2007

We think the more directions that architecture takes at this point, the better.

— Denise Scott Brown and Robert Venturi
Learning from Las Vegas, 1972

INTRODUCTION

The body of work that follows aims to fill the expanding gap between a profession that glorifies morphological originality through media exposure and a more secluded field of architectural research which, unlike its scientific counterparts, paradoxically neglects experimentation and the manipulation of form through its sole focus on writing. Proposing a creative alternative to critical academic literature, this study develops a prospective series of forms that focuses on the *nucleus* of architecture, the building as a unit (whether touched by others or left aside), and on the clarity of expression of its generative idea. As a result, in the coming chapters, *text* has radically been replaced by *form*.

In order to multiply the range of potentialities in architecture, this study accepts the physical aspect of buildings as its primary component (the periodic denial of which proving vain) and proceeds by trial and error. Rather than striving to identify a singular design method, it searches in as many directions as possible, then isolates a multitude of devices intended to differ from each other and to be open for further development. As a bank of ideas from which articles can be picked to fit particular sites and purposes, it embodies the desire to exceed the sum of concepts that come to mind when confronted with the overwhelming situation of an actual project.

The traditional sequence "program plus site equals form" is here intentionally inverted: as in ancient column orders, schemes are conceived prior to site insertion and subsequent relationships or adaptations. Yet beyond archaic dogmas, although a number of these figures constitute mere criticisms of recurrent paradigms in the discipline, most aspire to innovate and envision a more diverse future; to the point that many require construction techniques not available to date, if not different gravitational values.

In the absence of any given site, chapters are simply named after the locations from which the ideas they contain were conceived.

This chaotic sequence of places is employed to reveal a content that resists the primitive reaction of classification and thereby acknowledges the discontinuous nature of the creative process. Within a series that eventually generates its own context, scale—its a priori building material—is left to the imagination of the reader from one item to the next, with a range that can span from megastructure to cabin size.

For the sake of versatility, the illustrations of this series have been drawn freehand. What could appear as a deliberate reaction to the quasi-unanimous computerization of both architectural representation and building design process is, in fact, a simple choice of convenience. Not unlike the way physical modeling materials influence form, operating systems turn out to induce software-specific shapes, to the extent that they become barriers to the production of diversity. Making room for various layouts, freehand drawings have been reduced here to their most neutral expression, in order to minimize the input of the gestural and to extract the essence of the concept in its most intelligible formulation. This abatement of representational effects is extended to the adoption of a constant viewing angle, which, in turn, enhances the perception of both peculiarities and kinships.

In its layout, the present volume reproduces the graphic framework of a language. Not unlike the way a plurality of syllabaries cross each other in Japanese writing, several levels of character complexity are here juxtaposed with a quasi-absence of punctuation. Each entry is allocated the same amount of paper space (basically a square), whether extremely complicated (like *kanji*, or Chinese ideograms), simply curvy (like *hiragana*) or bluntly straight (like *katakana*). The parallel can be stretched to the reading experience itself, which can be carried out horizontally as well as vertically, and almost invariably from left to right or the reverse. Under each element though, captions, which in many cases preceded the drawings themselves, have been added to support or complete the depiction of their respective meanings.

Like a centrifugal escape from the cycle of serial fantasy, the last chapter reconnects with the cultural realities of an existing site in Japan, and becomes a scale test. Literally rescuing this opus from art book shelves, it exploits and shows the ability of this series to morph into proper building proportions with the outcome of a project, as the opposite of a conclusion. Selected for its median qualities in terms of size, program hosting capacities, and feasibility rather than for its demiurgical pretensions, a single scheme is released in the dense urban environment of central Tokyo to show the inherent flexibility that this set can offer. In return, this final part intends to reveal the *sitelessness* of all the other items by contrast.

CHAPTER ONE   **HONG KONG**

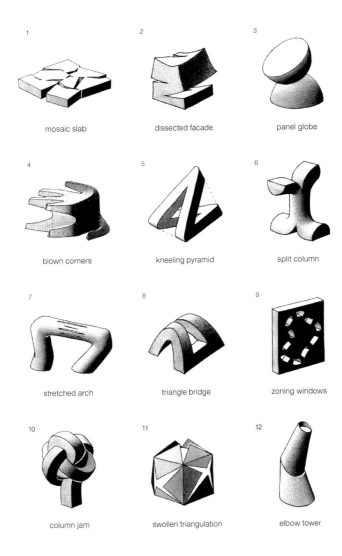

1 mosaic slab

2 dissected facade

3 panel globe

4 blown corners

5 kneeling pyramid

6 split column

7 stretched arch

8 triangle bridge

9 zoning windows

10 column jam

11 swollen triangulation

12 elbow tower

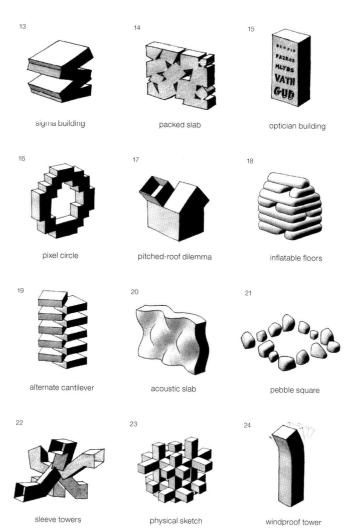

13

sigma building

14

packed slab

15

optician building

16

pixel circle

17

pitched-roof dilemma

18

inflatable floors

19

alternate cantilever

20

acoustic slab

21

pebble square

22

sleeve towers

23

physical sketch

24

windproof tower

4

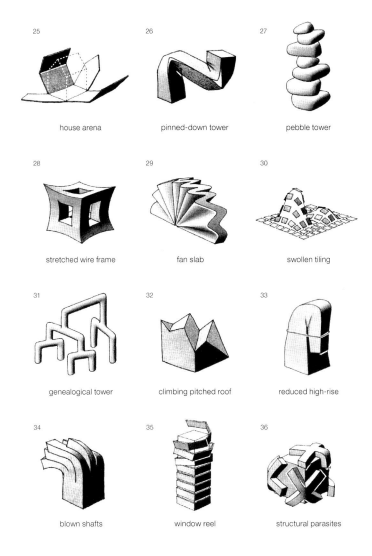

25
house arena

26
pinned-down tower

27
pebble tower

28
stretched wire frame

29
fan slab

30
swollen tiling

31
genealogical tower

32
climbing pitched roof

33
reduced high-rise

34
blown shafts

35
window reel

36
structural parasites

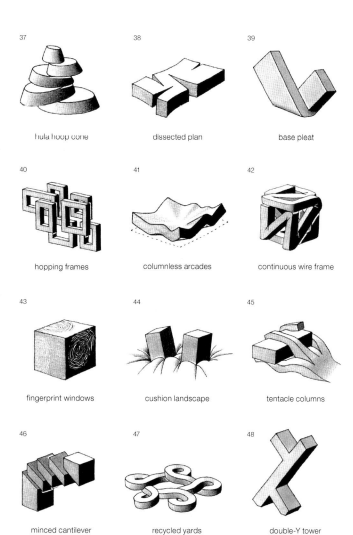

37	38	39
hula hoop cone	dissected plan	base pleat
40	41	42
hopping frames	columnless arcades	continuous wire frame
43	44	45
fingerprint windows	cushion landscape	tentacle columns
46	47	48
minced cantilever	recycled yards	double-Y tower

49

underground program

50

split building

51

courtyard splash

52

lava slab

53

seismic columns

54

skin = circulation

55

palm block

56

cone lanes

57

sphere cross

58

lifted halls

59

buoy structure

60

creeping tower

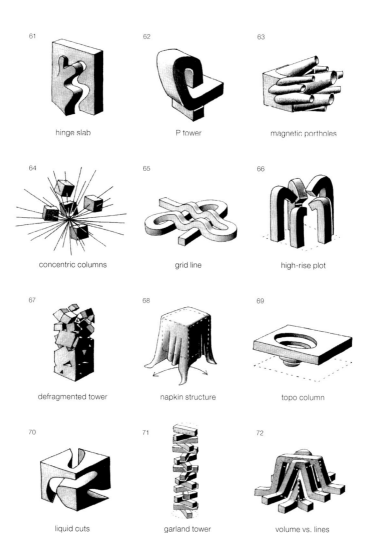

61
hinge slab

62
P tower

63
magnetic portholes

64
concentric columns

65
grid line

66
high-rise plot

67
defragmented tower

68
napkin structure

69
topo column

70
liquid cuts

71
garland tower

72
volume vs. lines

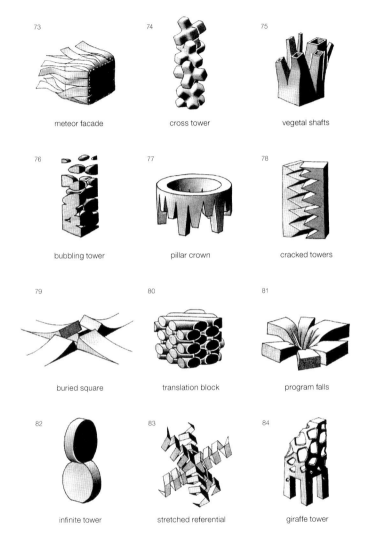

73 meteor facade

74 cross tower

75 vegetal shafts

76 bubbling tower

77 pillar crown

78 cracked towers

79 buried square

80 translation block

81 program falls

82 infinite tower

83 stretched referential

84 giraffe tower

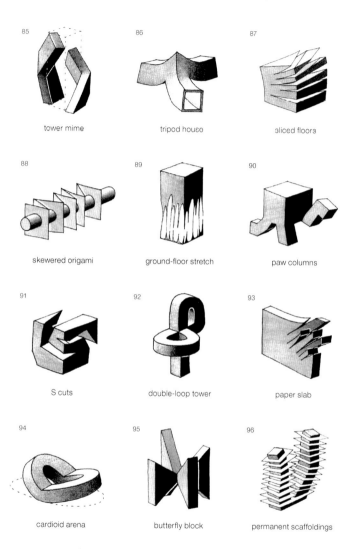

85 tower mime

86 tripod house

87 sliced floors

88 skewered origami

89 ground-floor stretch

90 paw columns

91 S cuts

92 double-loop tower

93 paper slab

94 cardioid arena

95 butterfly block

96 permanent scaffoldings

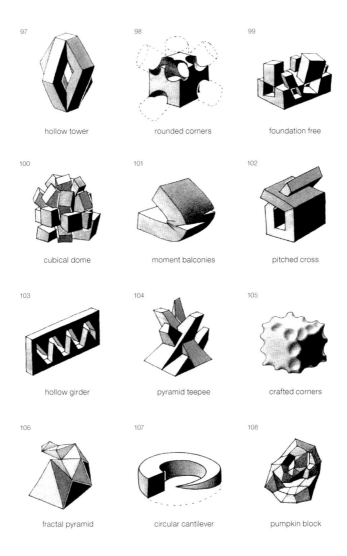

97
hollow tower

98
rounded corners

99
foundation free

100
cubical dome

101
moment balconies

102
pitched cross

103
hollow girder

104
pyramid teepee

105
crafted corners

106
fractal pyramid

107
circular cantilever

108
pumpkin block

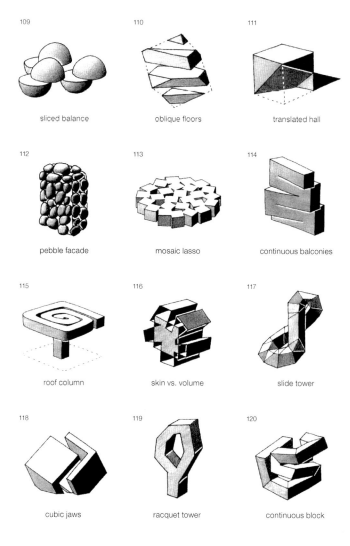

109
sliced balance

110
oblique floors

111
translated hall

112
pebble facade

113
mosaic lasso

114
continuous balconies

115
roof column

116
skin vs. volume

117
slide tower

118
cubic jaws

119
racquet tower

120
continuous block

121

global slabs

122

flake slab

123

milled portholes

124

bipolar block

125

compressed path

126

locked tower

127

stem towers

128

fiber program

129

pitched floors

130

hatched floors

131

digital slab

132

district tower

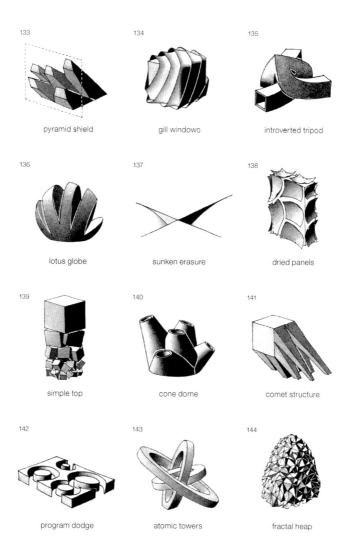

133
pyramid shield

134
gill windows

135
introverted tripod

136
lotus globe

137
sunken erasure

138
dried panels

139
simple top

140
cone dome

141
comet structure

142
program dodge

143
atomic towers

144
fractal heap

14

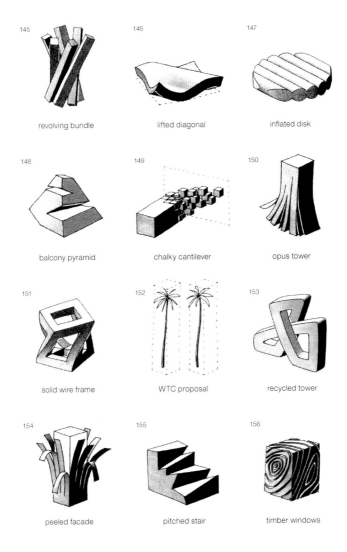

145 revolving bundle

146 lifted diagonal

147 inflated disk

148 balcony pyramid

149 chalky cantilever

150 opus tower

151 solid wire frame

152 WTC proposal

153 recycled tower

154 peeled facade

155 pitched stair

156 timber windows

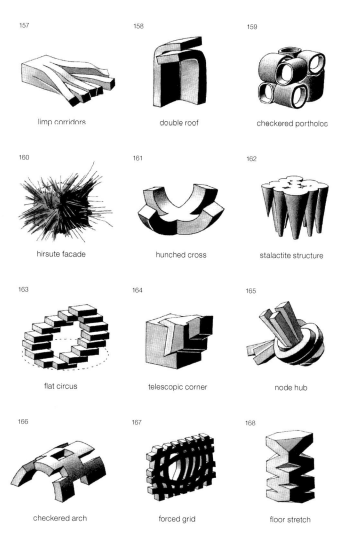

157
limp corridors

158
double roof

159
checkered portholes

160
hirsute facade

161
hunched cross

162
stalactite structure

163
flat circus

164
telescopic corner

165
node hub

166
checkered arch

167
forced grid

168
floor stretch

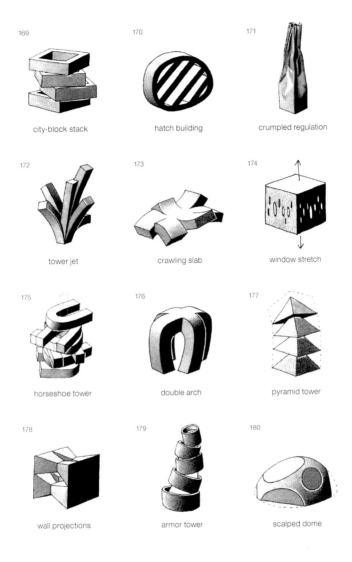

169

city-block stack

170

hatch building

171

crumpled regulation

172

tower jet

173

crawling slab

174

window stretch

175

horseshoe tower

176

double arch

177

pyramid tower

178

wall projections

179

armor tower

180

scalped dome

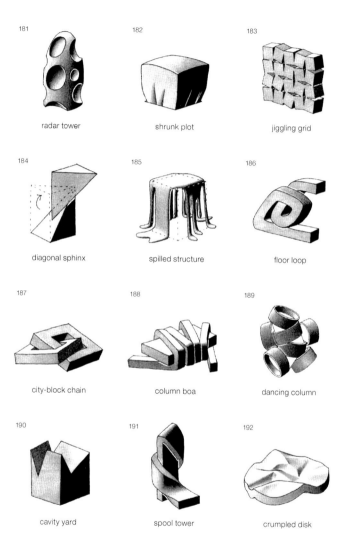

181
radar tower

182
shrunk plot

183
jiggling grid

184
diagonal sphinx

185
spilled structure

186
floor loop

187
city-block chain

188
column boa

189
dancing column

190
cavity yard

191
spool tower

192
crumpled disk

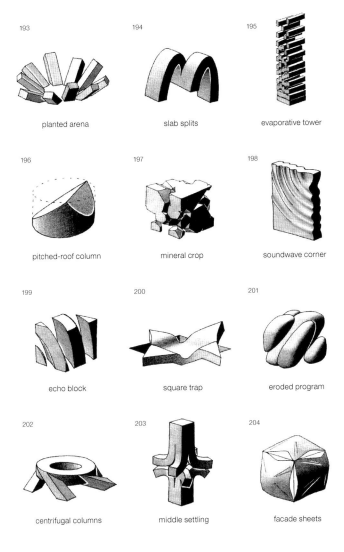

193

planted arena

194

slab splits

195

evaporative tower

196

pitched-roof column

197

mineral crop

198

soundwave corner

199

echo block

200

square trap

201

eroded program

202

centrifugal columns

203

middle settling

204

facade sheets

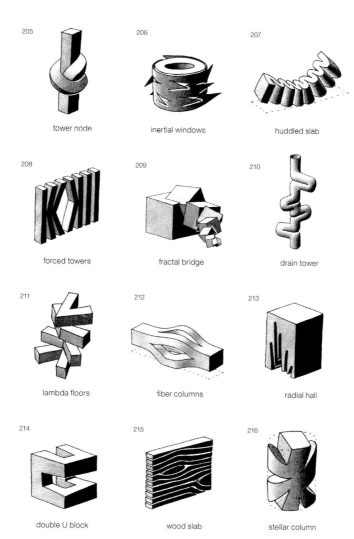

205 tower node

206 inertial windows

207 huddled slab

208 forced towers

209 fractal bridge

210 drain tower

211 lambda floors

212 fiber columns

213 radial hall

214 double U block

215 wood slab

216 stellar column

217

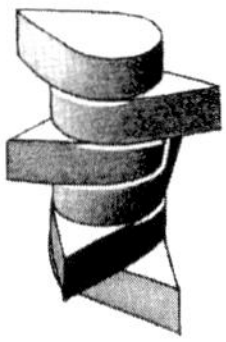

orientation tower

218

forensic housing

219

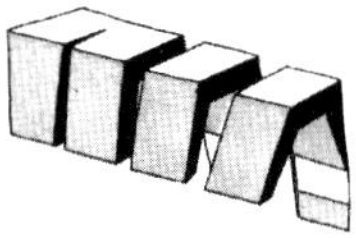

elastic block

220

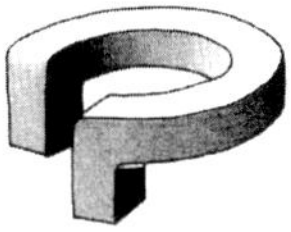

3/4 cantilever

221

Paris plan windows

222

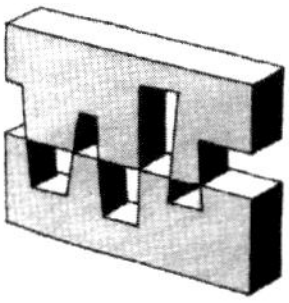

jaw slab

223

half-moon tower

224

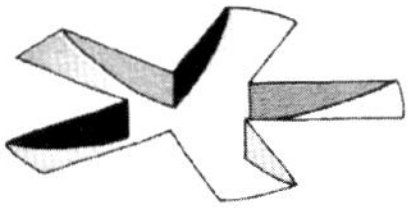

buried star

CHAPTER TWO   **NEW YORK**

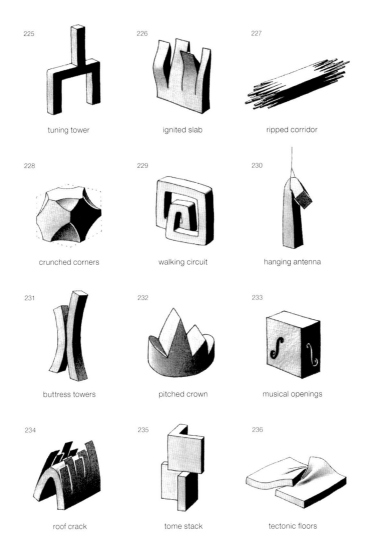

225 tuning tower

226 ignited slab

227 ripped corridor

228 crunched corners

229 walking circuit

230 hanging antenna

231 buttress towers

232 pitched crown

233 musical openings

234 roof crack

235 tome stack

236 tectonic floors

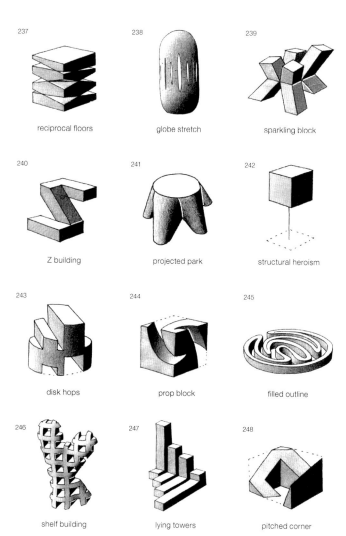

237   reciprocal floors

238   globe stretch

239   sparkling block

240   Z building

241   projected park

242   structural heroism

243   disk hops

244   prop block

245   filled outline

246   shelf building

247   lying towers

248   pitched corner

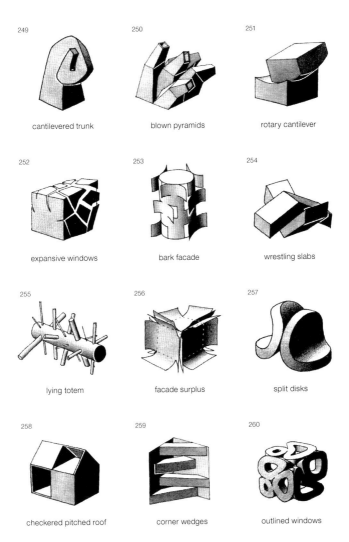

249
cantilevered trunk

250
blown pyramids

251
rotary cantilever

252
expansive windows

253
bark facade

254
wrestling slabs

255
lying totem

256
facade surplus

257
split disks

258
checkered pitched roof

259
corner wedges

260
outlined windows

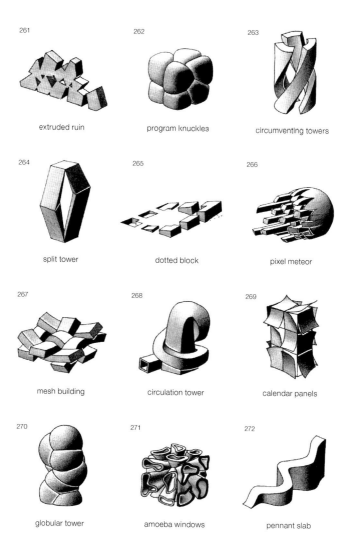

261
extruded ruin

262
program knuckles

263
circumventing towers

264
split tower

265
dotted block

266
pixel meteor

267
mesh building

268
circulation tower

269
calendar panels

270
globular tower

271
amoeba windows

272
pennant slab

273

pinecone flats

274

courtyard triangle

275

quartered globe

276

tamped cone

277

expanded block

278

chapped column

279

bifurcated balconies

280

floor hook

281

slalom structure

282

inverted ruin

283

radial facades

284

caryatid towers

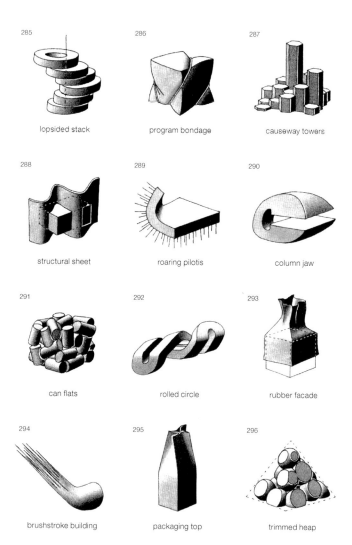

285

lopsided stack

286

program bondage

287

causeway towers

288

structural sheet

289

roaring pilotis

290

column jaw

291

can flats

292

rolled circle

293

rubber facade

294

brushstroke building

295

packaging top

296

trimmed heap

297

corner hubs

298

glowing square

299

dotted frame

300

dotted-marks tower

301

dry curtain walls

302

facade drag

303

square vs. tower

304

prop cantilever

305

flat curve

306

wrung city block

307

floor trap

308

barrel square

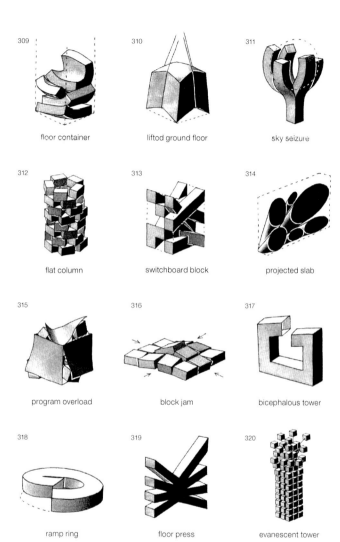

309   floor container

310   liftod ground floor

311   sky seizure

312   flat column

313   switchboard block

314   projected slab

315   program overload

316   block jam

317   bicephalous tower

318   ramp ring

319   floor press

320   evanescent tower

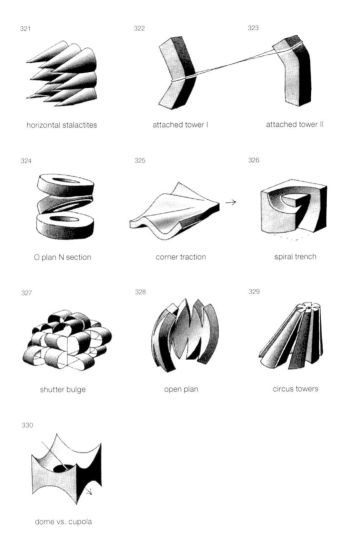

321 horizontal stalactites

322 attached tower I

323 attached tower II

324 O plan N section

325 corner traction

326 spiral trench

327 shutter bulge

328 open plan

329 circus towers

330 dome vs. cupola

CHAPTER THREE   **COPENHAGEN**

331

pentagon tower

332

fingerprint urbanism

333

cornet slab

334

oblique twist

335

finger-frame towers

336

foliate facades

337

ramified tower

338

star vs. square

339

volume simulacrum

340

open city block

341

medallion slab

342

XYZ megastructure

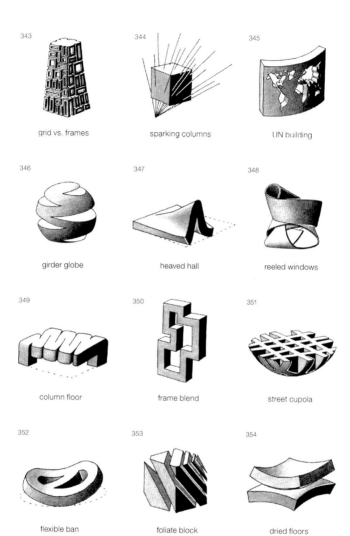

343 grid vs. frames

344 sparking columns

345 UN building

346 girder globe

347 heaved hall

348 reeled windows

349 column floor

350 frame blend

351 street cupola

352 flexible ban

353 foliate block

354 dried floors

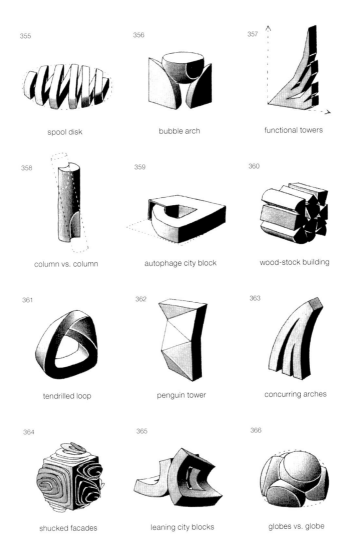

355

spool disk

356

bubble arch

357

functional towers

358

column vs. column

359

autophage city block

360

wood-stock building

361

tendrilled loop

362

penguin tower

363

concurring arches

364

shucked facades

365

leaning city blocks

366

globes vs. globe

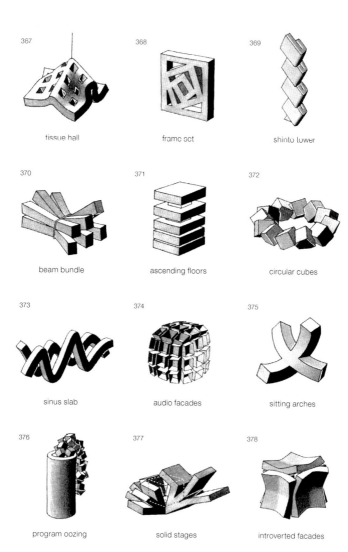

367
tissue hall

368
frame set

369
shinto tower

370
beam bundle

371
ascending floors

372
circular cubes

373
sinus slab

374
audio facades

375
sitting arches

376
program oozing

377
solid stages

378
introverted facades

floor bud

extruded zoning

beveled edges

cement slab

corner radiation

window film

extruded erasure

prop walls

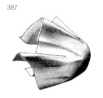

paper comet

fourfold floor

radius overlap

facade tension

underground arch

facade towers

homothetic square

corner tower

pinned column

magic pilotis

urban arch

tangential globe

dotted sequence

score windows

envelope building

canvas slab

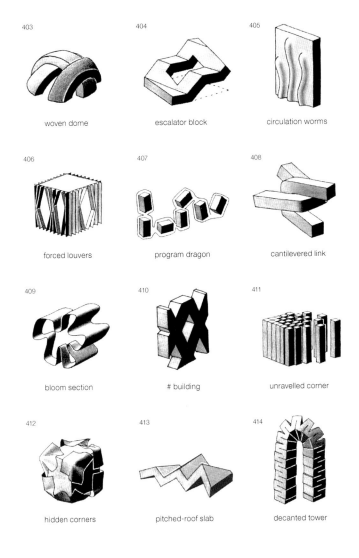

403
woven dome

404
escalator block

405
circulation worms

406
forced louvers

407
program dragon

408
cantilevered link

409
bloom section

410
building

411
unravelled corner

412
hidden corners

413
pitched-roof slab

414
decanted tower

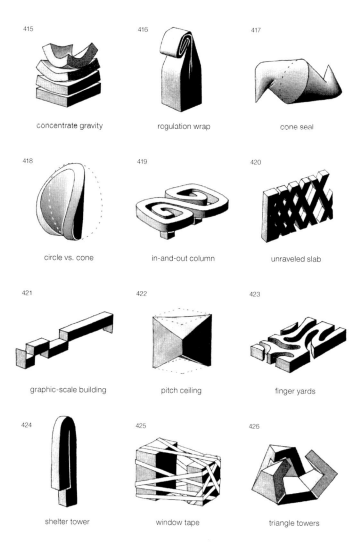

415
concentrate gravity

416
regulation wrap

417
cone seal

418
circle vs. cone

419
in-and-out column

420
unraveled slab

421
graphic-scale building

422
pitch ceiling

423
finger yards

424
shelter tower

425
window tape

426
triangle towers

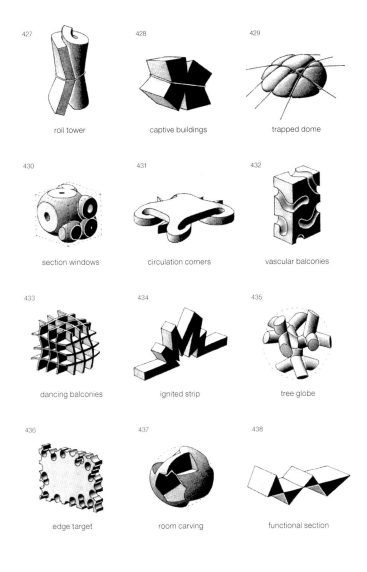

427
roll tower

428
captive buildings

429
trapped dome

430
section windows

431
circulation corners

432
vascular balconies

433
dancing balconies

434
ignited strip

435
tree globe

436
edge target

437
room carving

438
functional section

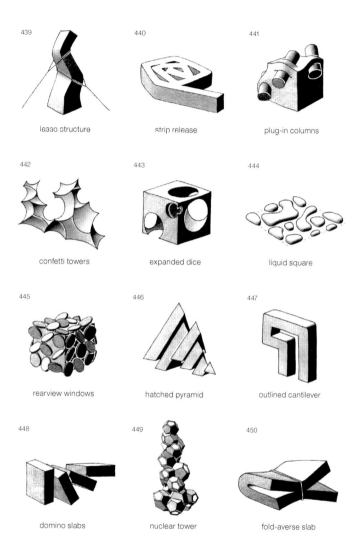

439

lasso structure

440

strip release

441

plug-in columns

442

confetti towers

443

expanded dice

444

liquid square

445

rearview windows

446

hatched pyramid

447

outlined cantilever

448

domino slabs

449

nuclear tower

450

fold-averse slab

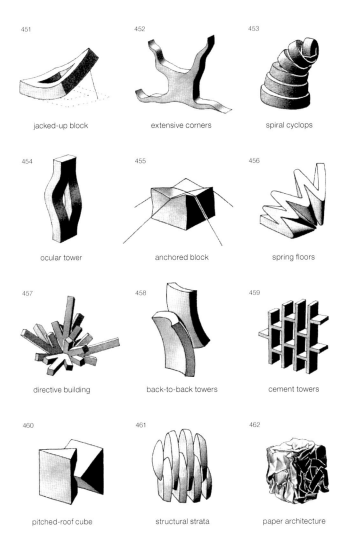

451 jacked-up block

452 extensive corners

453 spiral cyclops

454 ocular tower

455 anchored block

456 spring floors

457 directive building

458 back-to-back towers

459 cement towers

460 pitched-roof cube

461 structural strata

462 paper architecture

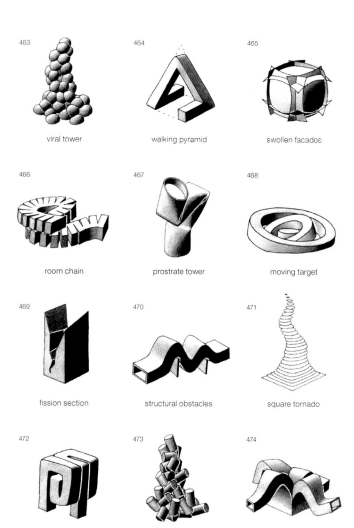

463

viral tower

464

walking pyramid

465

swollen facades

466

room chain

467

prostrate tower

468

moving target

469

fission section

470

structural obstacles

471

square tornado

472

continuous pillar

473

column heap

474

erupted pyramid

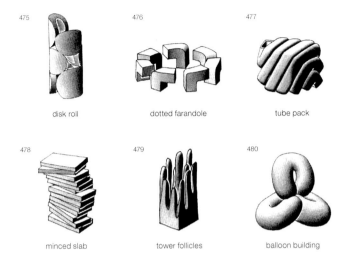

475

disk roll

476

dotted farandole

477

tube pack

478

minced slab

479

tower follicles

480

balloon building

CHAPTER FOUR   **LOS ANGELES**

481

olympic building

482

erected veil

483

linear vs. concentric

484

limp tripod

485

back-pass towers

486

capsule tree

487

underground towers

488

extruded camouflage

489

projected block

490

wheel tower

491

billboard floor

492

vertical zoo

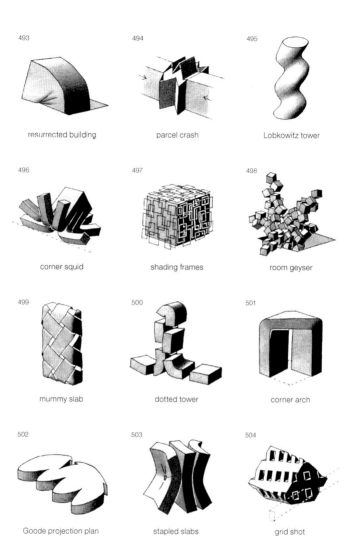

493
resurrected building

494
parcel crash

495
Lobkowitz tower

496
corner squid

497
shading frames

498
room geyser

499
mummy slab

500
dotted tower

501
corner arch

502
Goode projection plan

503
stapled slabs

504
grid shot

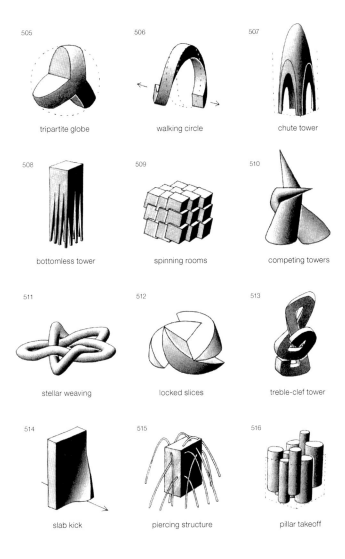

505

tripartite globe

506

walking circle

507

chute tower

508

bottomless tower

509

spinning rooms

510

competing towers

511

stellar weaving

512

locked slices

513

treble-clef tower

514

slab kick

515

piercing structure

516

pillar takeoff

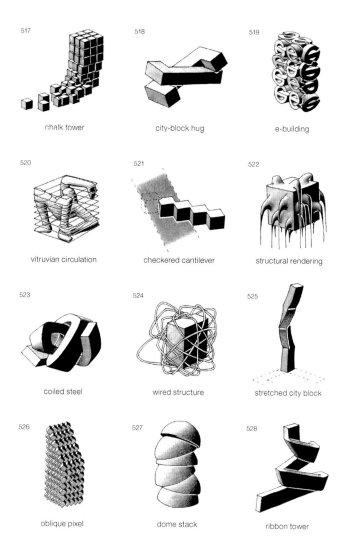

517 chalk tower

518 city-block hug

519 e-building

520 vitruvian circulation

521 checkered cantilever

522 structural rendering

523 coiled steel

524 wired structure

525 stretched city block

526 oblique pixel

527 dome stack

528 ribbon tower

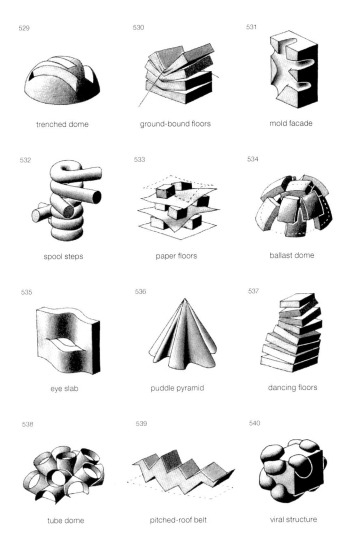

529
trenched dome

530
ground-bound floors

531
mold facade

532
spool steps

533
paper floors

534
ballast dome

535
eye slab

536
puddle pyramid

537
dancing floors

538
tube dome

539
pitched-roof belt

540
viral structure

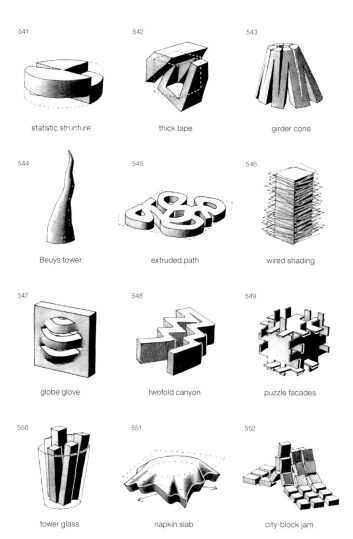

541

statistic structure

542

thick tape

543

girder cone

544

Beuys tower

545

extruded path

546

wired shading

547

globe glove

548

twofold canyon

549

puzzle facades

550

tower glass

551

napkin slab

552

city-block jam

553

ivy screen

554

tower arena

555

pillar stock

556

program glass

557

pyramid pennant

558

free Plan Voisin

559

convergent towers

560

dome plus

561

cube screw

562

log-joint building

563

cube hug

564

garland floors

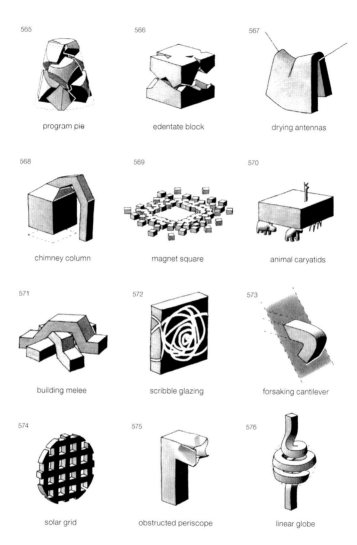

565
program pie

566
edentate block

567
drying antennas

568
chimney column

569
magnet square

570
animal caryatids

571
building melee

572
scribble glazing

573
forsaking cantilever

574
solar grid

575
obstructed periscope

576
linear globe

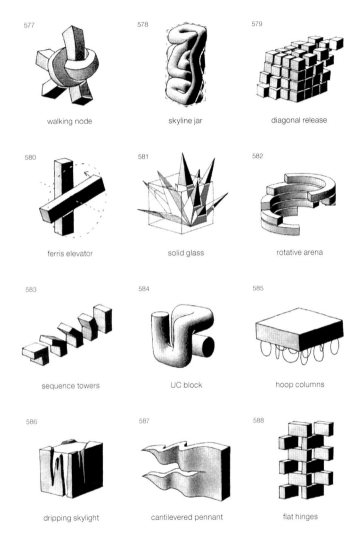

577
walking node

578
skyline jar

579
diagonal release

580
ferris elevator

581
solid glass

582
rotative arena

583
sequence towers

584
UC block

585
hoop columns

586
dripping skylight

587
cantilevered pennant

588
flat hinges

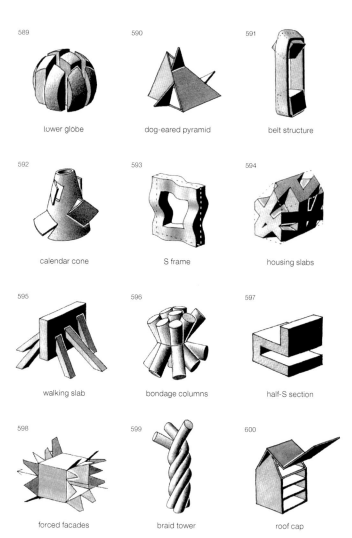

589

lower globe

590

dog-eared pyramid

591

belt structure

592

calendar cone

593

S frame

594

housing slabs

595

walking slab

596

bondage columns

597

half-S section

598

forced facades

599

braid tower

600

roof cap

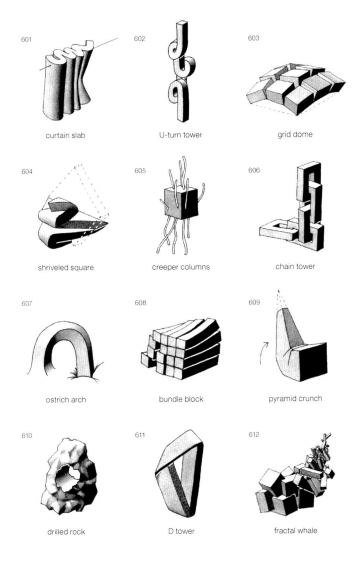

601   curtain slab

602   U-turn tower

603   grid dome

604   shriveled square

605   creeper columns

606   chain tower

607   ostrich arch

608   bundle block

609   pyramid crunch

610   drilled rock

611   D tower

612   fractal whale

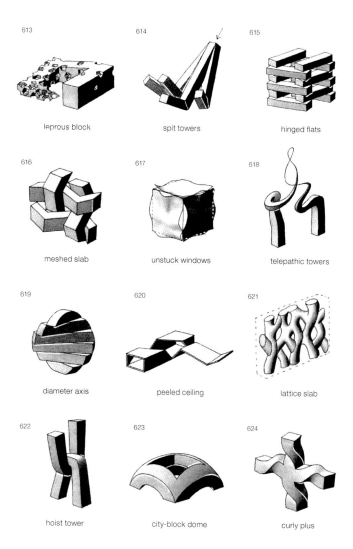

613
leprous block

614
spit towers

615
hinged flats

616
meshed slab

617
unstuck windows

618
telepathic towers

619
diameter axis

620
peeled ceiling

621
lattice slab

622
hoist tower

623
city-block dome

624
curly plus

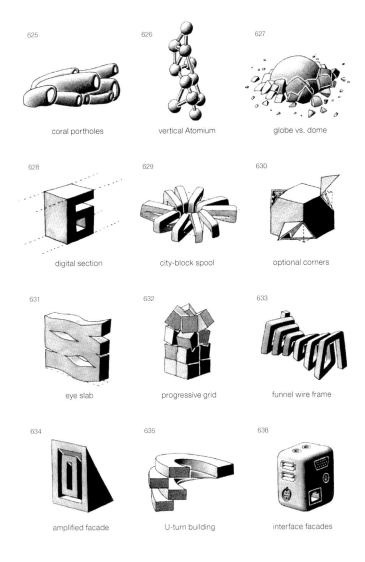

625

coral portholes

626

vertical Atomium

627

globe vs. dome

628

digital section

629

city-block spool

630

optional corners

631

eye slab

632

progressive grid

633

funnel wire frame

634

amplified facade

635

U-turn building

636

interface facades

637
global cross

638
collision crop

639
internal battle

640
topo facades

641
amoeba slab

642
pigtail towers

643
exponential balconies

644
finger-frame lock

645
program texture

646
horned corners

647
ticket tower

648
crown jaws

649 frame slab

650 wire-frame column

651 program potato

652 block hug

653 spiral bowl

654 cubical ivy

655 topo stairs

656 oblique wave

657 striped bowl

658 climbing balconies

659 corner columns

660 column jaws

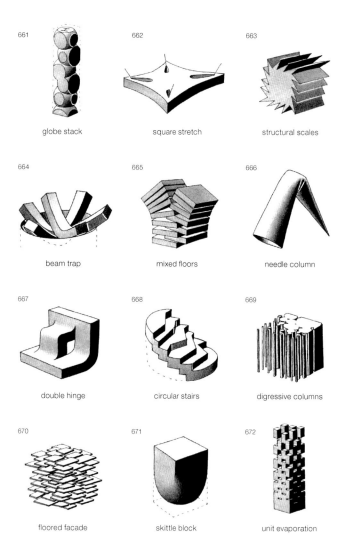

661 globe stack

662 square stretch

663 structural scales

664 beam trap

665 mixed floors

666 needle column

667 double hinge

668 circular stairs

669 digressive columns

670 floored facade

671 skittle block

672 unit evaporation

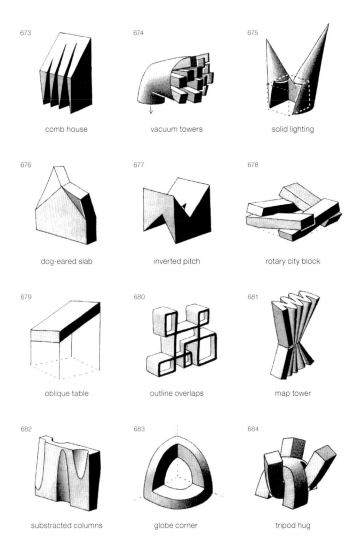

673
comb house

674
vacuum towers

675
solid lighting

676
dog-eared slab

677
inverted pitch

678
rotary city block

679
oblique table

680
outline overlaps

681
map tower

682
substracted columns

683
globe corner

684
tripod hug

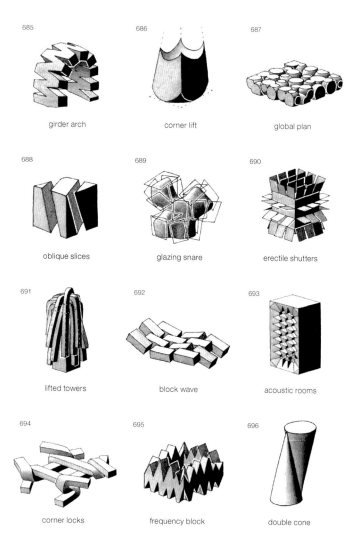

685

girder arch

686

corner lift

687

global plan

688

oblique slices

689

glazing snare

690

erectile shutters

691

lifted towers

692

block wave

693

acoustic rooms

694

corner locks

695

frequency block

696

double cone

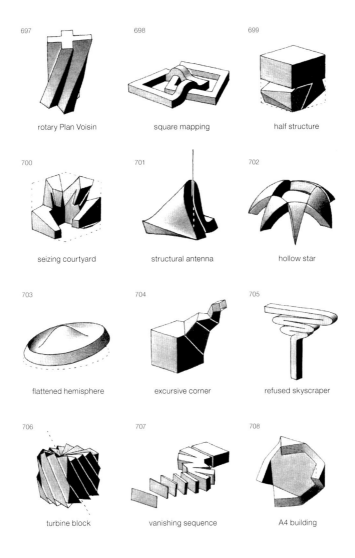

697 rotary Plan Voisin

698 square mapping

699 half structure

700 seizing courtyard

701 structural antenna

702 hollow star

703 flattened hemisphere

704 excursive corner

705 refused skyscraper

706 turbine block

707 vanishing sequence

708 A4 building

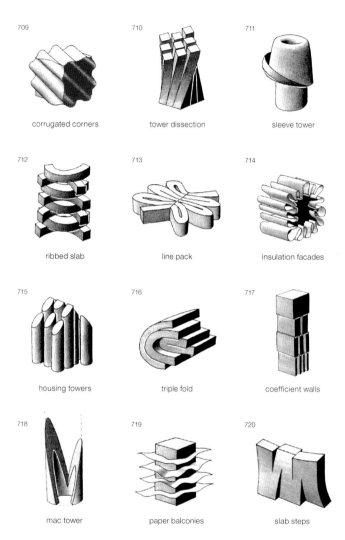

709
corrugated corners

710
tower dissection

711
sleeve tower

712
ribbed slab

713
line pack

714
insulation facades

715
housing towers

716
triple fold

717
coefficient walls

718
mac tower

719
paper balconies

720
slab steps

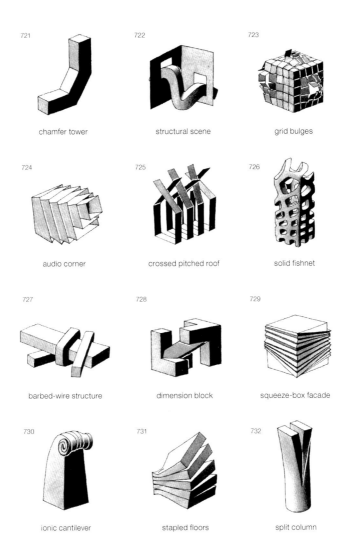

721 chamfer tower

722 structural scene

723 grid bulges

724 audio corner

725 crossed pitched roof

726 solid fishnet

727 barbed-wire structure

728 dimension block

729 squeeze-box facade

730 ionic cantilever

731 stapled floors

732 split column

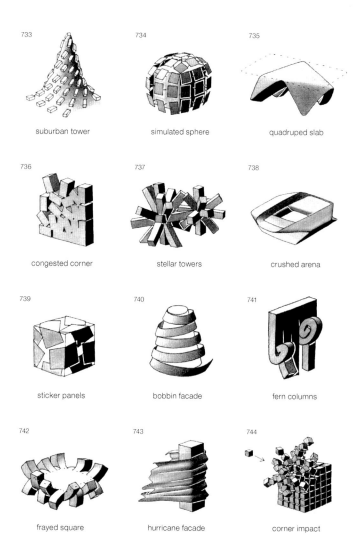

733

suburban tower

734

simulated sphere

735

quadruped slab

736

congested corner

737

stellar towers

738

crushed arena

739

sticker panels

740

bobbin facade

741

fern columns

742

frayed square

743

hurricane facade

744

corner impact

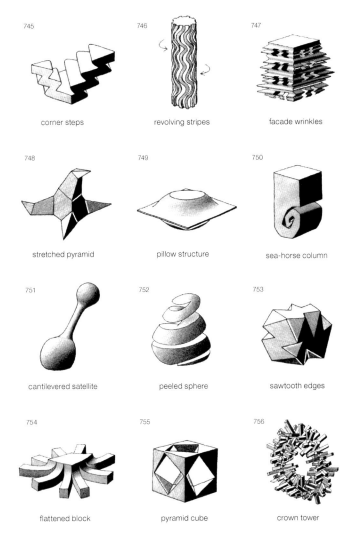

745

corner steps

746

revolving stripes

747

facade wrinkles

748

stretched pyramid

749

pillow structure

750

sea-horse column

751

cantilevered satellite

752

peeled sphere

753

sawtooth edges

754

flattened block

755

pyramid cube

756

crown tower

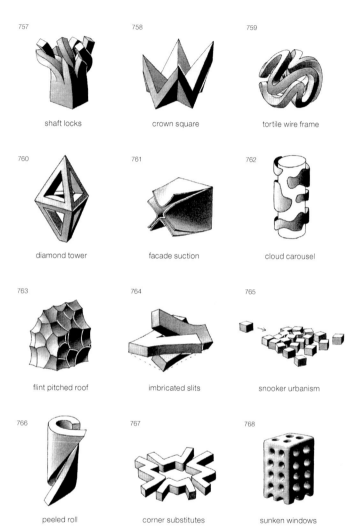

757
shaft locks

758
crown square

759
tortile wire frame

760
diamond tower

761
facade suction

762
cloud carousel

763
flint pitched roof

764
imbricated slits

765
snooker urbanism

766
peeled roll

767
corner substitutes

768
sunken windows

769

dried grid

770

stamen block

771

XXX floors

772

telescopic city block

773

landed Sputnik

774

corner cloud

775

crisscross sections

CHAPTER FIVE   **TOKYO**

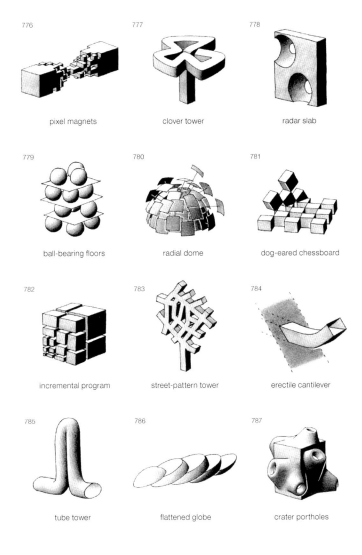

776 pixel magnets

777 clover tower

778 radar slab

779 ball-bearing floors

780 radial dome

781 dog-eared chessboard

782 incremental program

783 street-pattern tower

784 erectile cantilever

785 tube tower

786 flattened globe

787 crater portholes

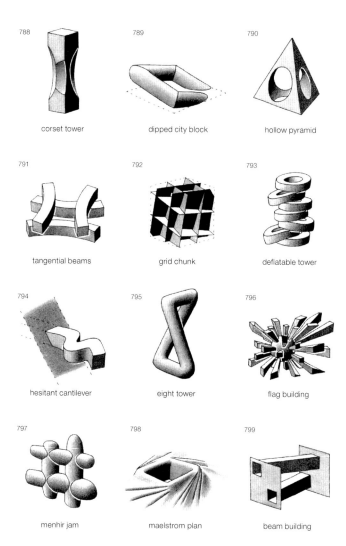

788 corset tower

789 dipped city block

790 hollow pyramid

791 tangential beams

792 grid chunk

793 deflatable tower

794 hesitant cantilever

795 eight tower

796 flag building

797 menhir jam

798 maelstrom plan

799 beam building

800

twig square

801

flaccid edges

802

stealth circle

803

bundletower

804

structural hub

805

akimbo tower

806

pyramid blimp

807

global tower

808

splash towers

809

modern buttresses

810

columnless floors

811

bumped geode

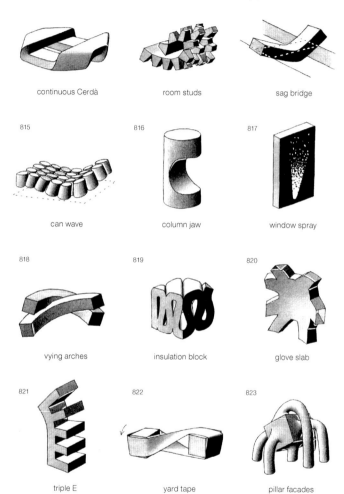

812

continuous Cerdà

813

room studs

814

sag bridge

815

can wave

816

column jaw

817

window spray

818

vying arches

819

insulation block

820

glove slab

821

triple E

822

yard tape

823

pillar facades

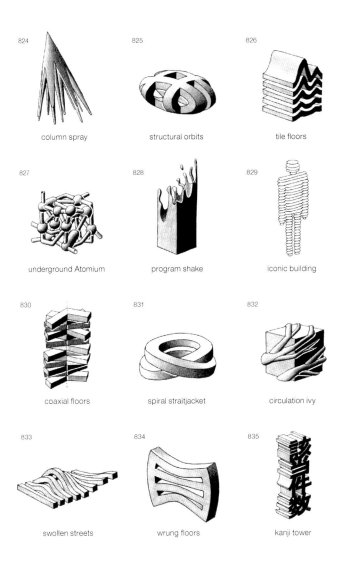

824

column spray

825

structural orbits

826

tile floors

827

underground Atomium

828

program shake

829

iconic building

830

coaxial floors

831

spiral straitjacket

832

circulation ivy

833

swollen streets

834

wrung floors

835

kanji tower

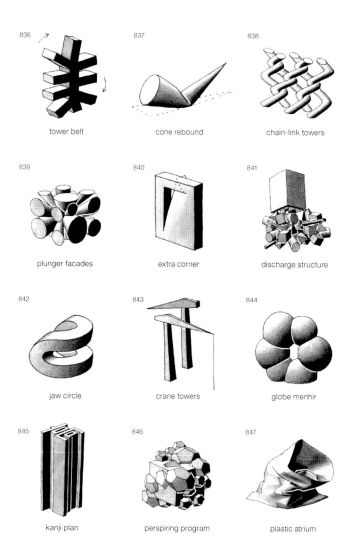

836 tower belt

837 cone rebound

838 chain-link towers

839 plunger facades

840 extra corner

841 discharge structure

842 jaw circle

843 crane towers

844 globe menhir

845 kanji plan

846 perspiring program

847 plastic atrium

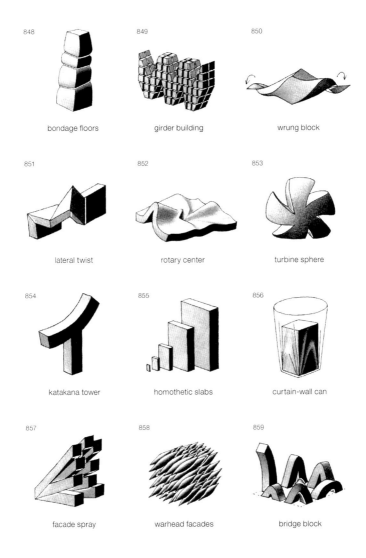

848 bondage floors

849 girder building

850 wrung block

851 lateral twist

852 rotary center

853 turbine sphere

854 katakana tower

855 homothetic slabs

856 curtain-wall can

857 facade spray

858 warhead facades

859 bridge block

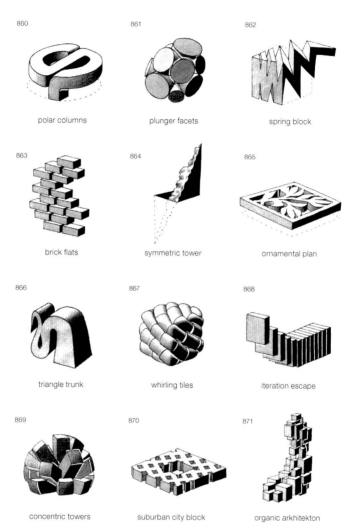

860

polar columns

861

plunger facets

862

spring block

863

brick flats

864

symmetric tower

865

ornamental plan

866

triangle trunk

867

whirling tiles

868

iteration escape

869

concentric towers

870

suburban city block

871

organic arkhitekton

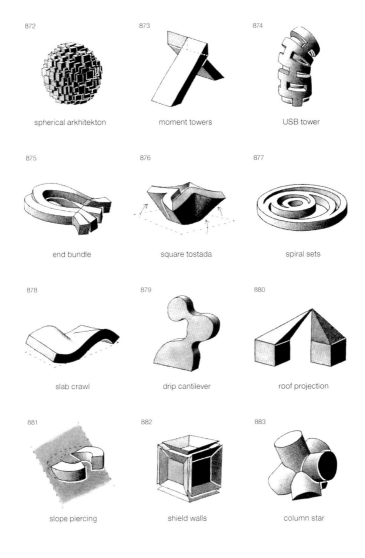

872
spherical arkhitekton

873
moment towers

874
USB tower

875
end bundle

876
square tostada

877
spiral sets

878
slab crawl

879
drip cantilever

880
roof projection

881
slope piercing

882
shield walls

883
column star

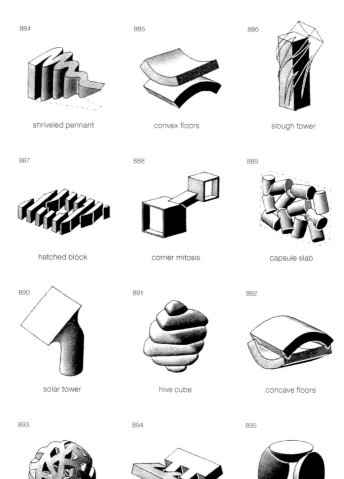

884
shriveled pennant

885
convex floors

886
slough tower

887
hatched block

888
corner mitosis

889
capsule slab

890
solar tower

891
hive cube

892
concave floors

893
lattice globe

894
hinged slab

895
radar arch

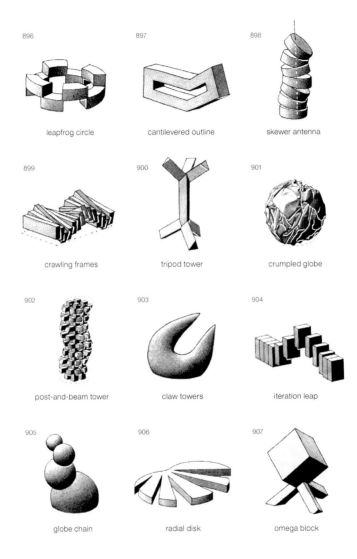

896
leapfrog circle

897
cantilevered outline

898
skewer antenna

899
crawling frames

900
tripod tower

901
crumpled globe

902
post-and-beam tower

903
claw towers

904
iteration leap

905
globe chain

906
radial disk

907
omega block

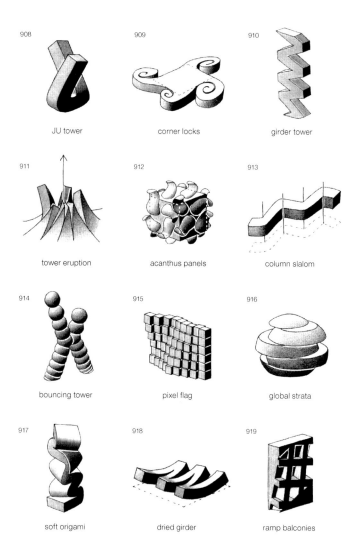

908

JU tower

909

corner locks

910

girder tower

911

tower eruption

912

acanthus panels

913

column slalom

914

bouncing tower

915

pixel flag

916

global strata

917

soft origami

918

dried girder

919

ramp balconies

920
siamese floors

921
deep billboard

922
cuff circle

923
centrifugal balconies

924
score building

925
canopy slide

926
extension icicles

927
fungal balconies

928
eye beam

929
glass meiosis

930
slab lock

931
radial column

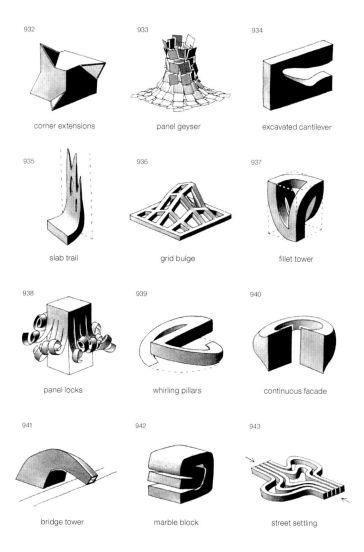

932
corner extensions

933
panel geyser

934
excavated cantilever

935
slab trail

936
grid bulge

937
fillet tower

938
panel locks

939
whirling pillars

940
continuous facade

941
bridge tower

942
marble block

943
street settling

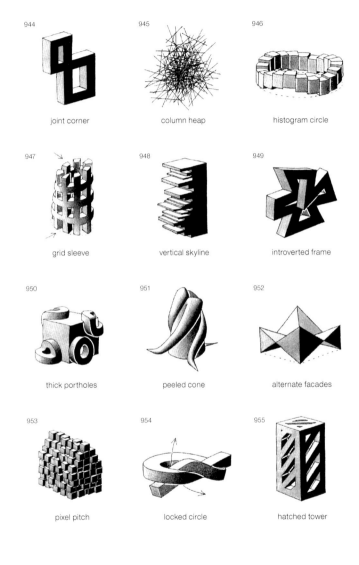

944
joint corner

945
column heap

946
histogram circle

947
grid sleeve

948
vertical skyline

949
introverted frame

950
thick portholes

951
peeled cone

952
alternate facades

953
pixel pitch

954
locked circle

955
hatched tower

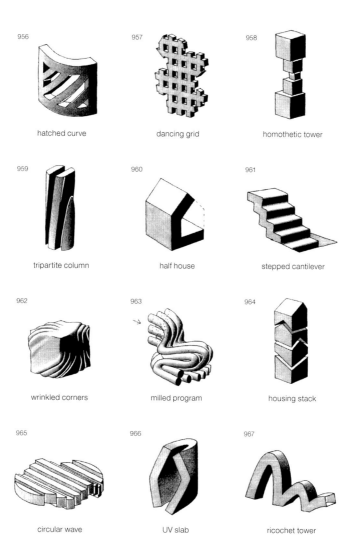

956
hatched curve

957
dancing grid

958
homothetic tower

959
tripartite column

960
half house

961
stepped cantilever

962
wrinkled corners

963
milled program

964
housing stack

965
circular wave

966
UV slab

967
ricochet tower

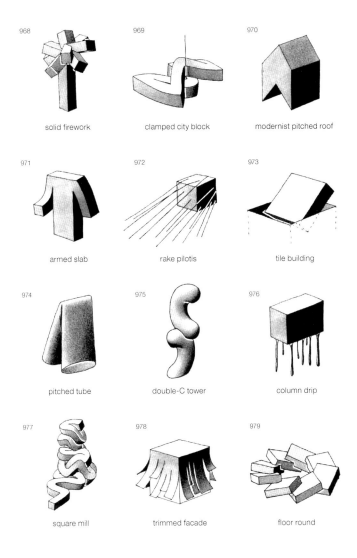

968
solid firework

969
clamped city block

970
modernist pitched roof

971
armed slab

972
rake pilotis

973
tile building

974
pitched tube

975
double-C tower

976
column drip

977
square mill

978
trimmed facade

979
floor round

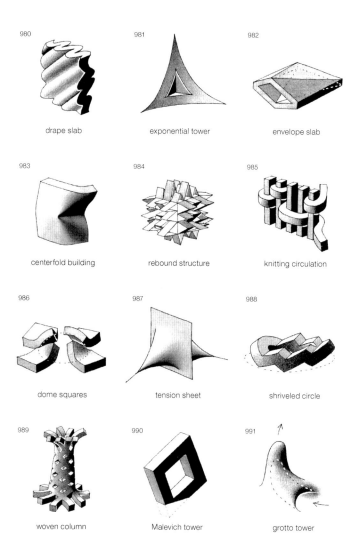

980
drape slab

981
exponential tower

982
envelope slab

983
centerfold building

984
rebound structure

985
knitting circulation

986
dome squares

987
tension sheet

988
shriveled circle

989
woven column

990
Malevich tower

991
grotto tower

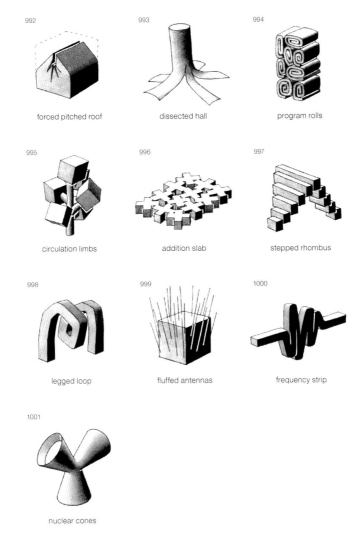

992

forced pitched roof

993

dissected hall

994

program rolls

995

circulation limbs

996

addition slab

997

stepped rhombus

998

legged loop

999

fluffed antennas

1000

frequency strip

1001

nuclear cones

CHAPTER SIX   **SCALE TEST**

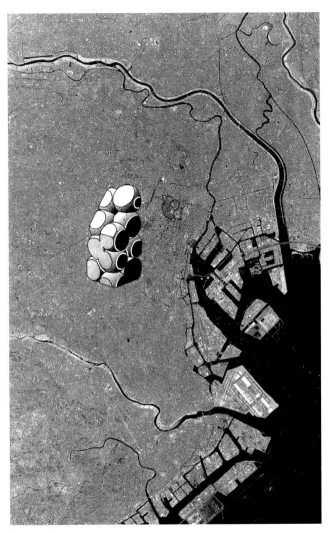

Tokyo as testbed

A tangential leap from the fantastical into reality, this final chapter explores the possibility of implementing a single scheme from the previous series (figure 638) as a building. Formerly inspired by Tokyo's rigid regulation system, the selected concept reconnects with the actual constraints of a site in that very city, landing on a plot adjacent to Yoyogi Park. The building—a usual combination of commercial, residential, and office spaces—is the result of the collision of twenty-three spheres (coincidentally equaling the number of Tokyo wards) of identical radius, which fuse inward to differentiate various spaces by vaults rather than walls. The seemingly random stacking of these elements allows groupings to create larger rooms when appropriate or divisions into smaller ones when cut by inner floors.

The remaining outer membrane of the structure is cropped as it meets the boundary defined by city building rules, thus providing diverse diameters of openings to match the respective functions and locations of the rooms. Facades become sections, leaving the appearance of the whole as a mere by-product of a compelled site-specificity.

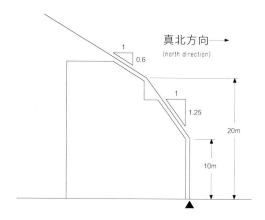

Zone 3 height regulation system from Shibuya City Office

Process model

0 10   50   100m

N

Urban situation

Aerial view

Street-level view

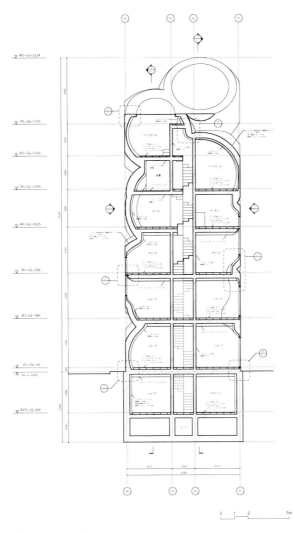

Transversal section

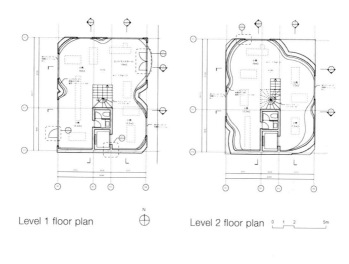

Level 1 floor plan

N

Level 2 floor plan   0 1 2   5m

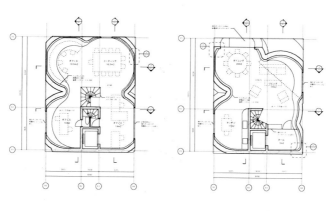

Level 3 floor plan

Level 4 floor plan

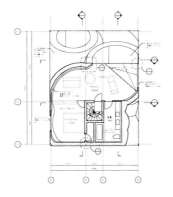

Level 5 floor plan

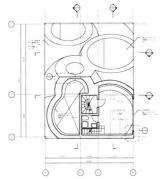

Level 6 floor plan

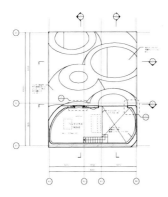

Level 7 floor plan

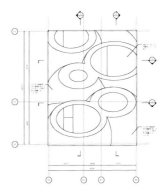

Roof plan

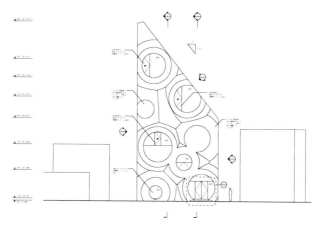

East elevation

0 1 2   5m

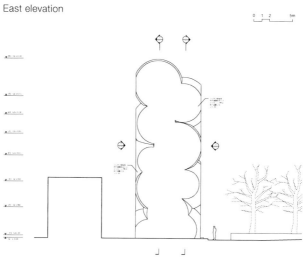

South elevation

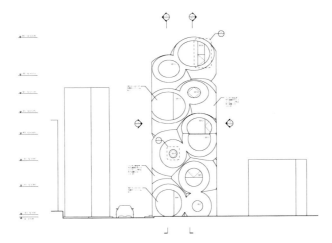

North elevation

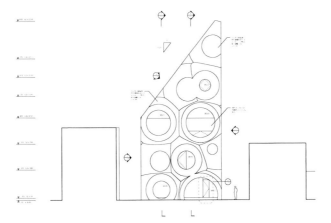

West elevation

View from Odakyu Line

CREDITS

Book design

François Blanciak
Hans Park

Project contributors

Wan-Ling Ko
Dick Olango
Omoi Toyonaga

Illustrations

NASA: 103
Shibuya City Office: 104
All other illustrations © François Blanciak